100 THINGS TO DO IN HARTFORD BEFORE YOU DIE

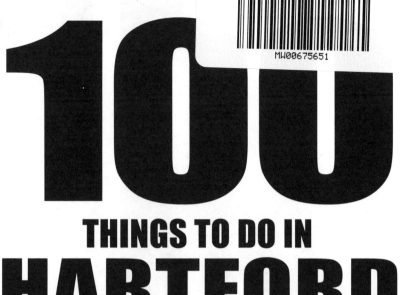

OMG

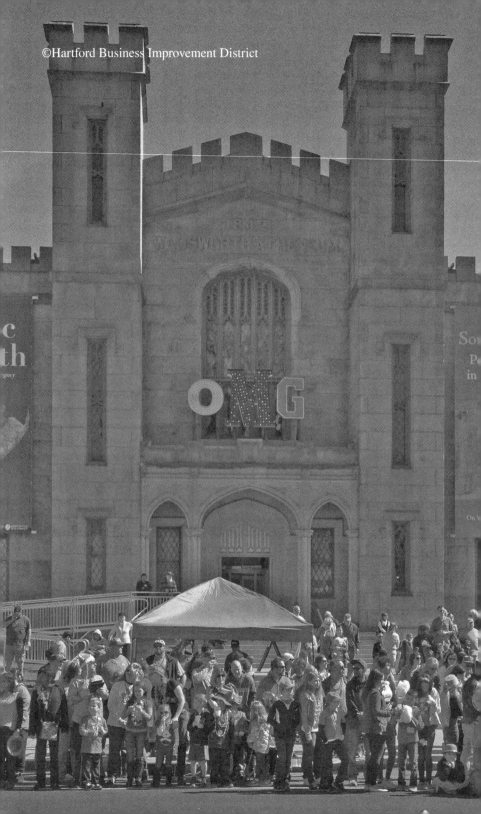

100 THINGS TO DO IN HARTFORD BEFORE YOU DIE

CHIP McCABE

REEDY PRESS

Reedy Press
PO Box 5131
St. Louis, MO 63139, USA
www.reedypress.com

Library of Congress Control Number: 9781681060873

ISBN: 2016958705

Design by Jill Halpin

Printed in the United States of America
17 18 19 20 21   5 4 3 2 1

Please note that websites, phone numbers, addresses, and company names are subject to change or cancellation. We did our best to relay the most accurate information available, but due to circumstances beyond our control, please do not hold us liable for misinformation. When exploring new destinations, please do your homework before you go.

DEDICATION

To those who wish to bloom wherever they are planted . . .

CONTENTS

Preface xiii

Acknowledgments xv

Food and Drink

1. Fill Up on Falafel (and More) at Tangiers 2
2. Eat Korean Barbeque at Sunberry 3
3. Enjoy a Farm-to-Table Meal at Firebox 4
4. Take a Tour of Latin American Cuisine in One Stop 6
5. Eat Thai Food in a Converted Living Room 7
6. Spoil Your Dinner with Italian Cookies and Pastries at Mozzicato's 8
7. Have Breakfast or Brunch at Mo's Midtown 10
8. Grab a Pint at Vaughan's Public House 12
9. Eat at the Polish National Home 13
10. Grab Some Sushi at Feng 14
11. Have a Drink at Little River Restoratives 16
12. Go Vegan (or Vegetarian) at Fire & Spice 17
13. Eat a Big Amount of Little Donuts 18
14. Linger over Tea or Coffee (or Something Else) at Tisane 19
15. Mangiare a Sorella 20
16. Visit Scotts' Jamaican Bakery 22
17. Sip Wine at Bin228 23
18. Grab a Beer at City Steam 24

19. Fill Up at Bear's Smokehouse 26
20. Plan a Week of Mexican Eats 27
21. Stock Up on Pasta at Difiore 28
22. Have a Beer at the Spigot 29
23. Visit the Spanish Coastline via Costa del Sol 30
24. Attend a Know Good Market 31
25. Experience a Meal at On20 32
26. Experience a Taste of Peru at Piolin 33
27. Take a Tour of Hartford Flavor Company 34
28. Experience a Taste of Colombia at La Fonda 35
29. Grab a Dog at Woody's 36
30. Get a Quick Bite at One of The Kitchens 37
31. Make a Stop at the First & Last Tavern 38
32. Grab a Grinder from Franklin Giant Sandwich Shop 40
33. Experience Ethiopian Cuisine at Abyssinian 41
34. Stop by the Hanging Hills Tasting Room 42
35. Spend an Evening at the Russell 43
36. Purchase Some Sausage from LaRosa's 44
37. Have Brunch at the Place 2 Be 45
38. Get in the Buffet Line at Brazil Grill 46
39. Spend an Evening at Casona 47

Music and Entertainment

40. Experience a Show at the Bushnell 50

41. Immerse Yourself in Improv 51

42. Make Monday Fun with Free Jazz in the Park 52

43. Visit the Charter Oak Cultural Center 53

44. See a Show at Hartford Stage 54

45. See a Show at TheaterWorks, Too 55

46. Get the Blues at Black-Eyed Sally's 56

47. Acquire a New Appreciation for Opera 57

48. Heed the Call of the Pipes 58

49. Enjoy the Music at Infinity Hall 59

50. Experience a Tnmot Aztro Performance 60

51. Attend a Hartford Symphony Orchestra Performance 61

52. Attend the Greater Hartford Festival of Jazz 63

53. See a Film at Cinestudio 64

54. Experience a Show at HartBeat Ensemble 65

55. Attend a Performance at the Academy of the Arts 66

56. Chill at the Black-Eyed & Blues Fest 67

57. Hit Up a Comic-Con, or Two 68

58. Attend a Hartt School Performance 69

59. Hang Out at Sully's Pub 70

60. Experience the Trinity International Hip-Hop Festival 72

61. Attend a Film Festival, or Two 73

62. Celebrate Hartford and a Hooker 75

Sports and Recreation

63. Race in the Art Sled Derby 78
64. Ice Skate in Bushnell Park during Winterfest 79
65. Ride the Bushnell Park Carousel 81
66. Spend the Day in Elizabeth Park 82
67. Cruise along the Connecticut River 83
68. Cheer on the Huskies at a UCONN Basketball Game 84
69. Attend a Wolf Pack Game 85
70. Play a Round at Goodwin and Keney Park Golf Courses 86
71. Watch a Vintage Baseball Game 87
72. Take a Stroll through Bushnell Park 89

Culture and History

73. Visit the Oldest Continuously Operating Public Art Museum 92
74. Tour the Home of Mark Twain 95
75. Spend the Day at Cedar Hill Cemetery 96
76. Watch the Dragon Boat Races and Take in the Asian Festival 99
77. Play with all the Stuff at the Connecticut Science Center 101
78. Embrace the Arts at Real Art Ways 102
79. Be Amazed by the Beauty of Night Fall 104
80. Read the Bricks on Pratt Street 105
81. Attend (or March in) a Parade 106
82. Visit the Harriet Beecher Stowe Center 107
83. Get a Taste of the Caribbean 108
84. Tour the Arch in Bushnell Park 109
85. Take a Sculpture Walk 111

86. Visit the Butler-McCook House 113
87. Visit EBK Gallery 114
88. Visit the Oldest Historic Site in Hartford 115
89. Take a Tour of the State Capitol 116
90. Tour the Connecticut Historical Society Museum 117
91. Visit the Joseloff Gallery 118
92. Explore the Museum of Connecticut History 119
93. Tour the Coltsville National Historic Park 120
94. Visit the Hartford History Center at the Library 121

Shopping and Fashion

95. Shop Local at Hartford Prints! 124
96. Attend the Trashion Fashion Show 126
97. Purchase Jeans that Will Last a Lifetime 127
98. Step Up to the (Camera) Bar 128
99. Treat Yourself at a Fashion Landmark 129
100. Slip into a Pair from the Brothers Crisp 130

Suggested Itineraries 131
Events by Season 137
Index 139

PREFACE

You see the expression plastered on banners, on stickers, as a hashtag on thousands of social media posts, and on the home page of Hartford.com—Hartford Has It. No truer statement was ever written about Connecticut's capital city. Hartford has a lot of awesome crammed into such a small geographic area. (The city proper constitutes about only eighteen square miles.) For a city that boasts only about 125,000 full-time residents, Hartford has an embarrassment of riches in the arts, dining, entertainment, history, and culture. Indeed, Hartford Has It.

What you are holding in your hands is exactly what the title says—it is 100 things to experience in Hartford while you still can. It is by no means a be-all, end-all type of list. But it is a very comprehensive look at the people, places, events, and things that make Hartford such a special place. You, dear reader, are more than encouraged to go out and eat all the food, attend all the events, and soak up all the history and culture that Hartford has to offer. Hartford has an open-door policy for those willing to experience the city in full.

Whether you're an adventure seeker already living in the greater Hartford area or a first time visitor, *100 Things to Do in Hartford Before You Die* will serve as your guide and trusty companion for touring one of the best little cities around. I hope you have as much fun exploring Hartford as I did writing about it.

As of the writing of this book all information is accurate. Sometimes things change, though. It's always recommended to call ahead or check websites before venturing out to your intended destination.

For an insider look on the city of Hartford, I highly recommend that you follow the Hartford.com Instagram feed at @hartfordhasit and Twitter feed at @hartforddotcom. You can also follow me on Twitter at @themetaldadblog and Instagram at @the_metal_dad.

Chip McCabe

ACKNOWLEDGMENTS

This book would not have been possible without the invaluable input of Jordan Polon, executive director of the Hartford Business Improvement District. Thanks also go out to friends and family who so willingly offered up their favorite Hartford spots any time the writing of this book came up in conversation. Your love of Hartford has been inspiring from day one. Thank you to my wife, Clover, for all her support and our four beautiful children, who keep their dad company on so many field trips.

FOOD AND DRINK

1

FILL UP ON FALAFEL (AND MORE) AT TANGIERS

On Farmington Avenue, roughly halfway between the town centers of Hartford and West Hartford, sits a somewhat nondescript brick building with a FedEx store and a Bank of America branch facing the street. But head around toward the back of the building and you'll discover what is arguably the best falafel in the state of Connecticut. The family-owned Tangiers International Market has been a foodie's paradise in Hartford for over twenty years, an oasis of international flavors spanning the entire Mediterranean region. It's one part market, featuring local produce and unique, hard-to-find items, and one part café, featuring freshly prepared salads, sandwiches, and entrees. Tangiers is the definition of a one-stop shop. Weekly grocery shopping aside, Tangiers is well worth the visit for its hearty menu filled with gyros, kebabs, stuffed eggplant dishes, and—of course—the best falafel in town, bar none.

550 Farmington Ave., 860-233-8168
TangiersMarket.com

2

EAT KOREAN BARBEQUE
AT SUNBERRY

Sunberry Café and Catering has a wide array of delicious choices on its menu: burgers, signature sandwiches, panini, wraps, and all-day breakfast options, just to name a few. But the best section of the menu includes the authentic Korean dishes. The Udon, Ramen, and Bibimbap dishes are all highly recommended specialties you won't find in many other places in town. But it's the Korean-style barbeque dishes that really knock it out of the park, with massive portions and amazingly fresh veggies sautéed to perfection over an open flame. It's the perfect pit stop for breakfast or lunch if you happen to be downtown for work or an event at one of the many attractions within walking distance.

65 Pratt St., 860-241-0811
hartford.com/sunberry

3

ENJOY A FARM-TO-TABLE MEAL AT FIREBOX

Nestled in the Frog Hollow section of Hartford is Firebox Restaurant, a unique farm-to-table dining experience. Since they opened in 2007, they've been fully committed to providing delicious ways to present locally sourced cuisine. From extraordinary salads to hormone-free meats to some of the best hand-cut French fries you'll ever experience, Firebox has a wide array of options to appease even the most discerning palates. Serving both lunch and dinner amongst beautiful décor and stocked with a full bar, Firebox can be the perfect mid-day break or part of a romantic evening out. A meal at Firebox not only does your taste buds good, but also benefits the local community as well. Profits from the restaurant go to support Billings Forge Community Works, a driving force for community participation and empowerment.

539 Broad St., 860-246-1222
fireboxrestaurant.com

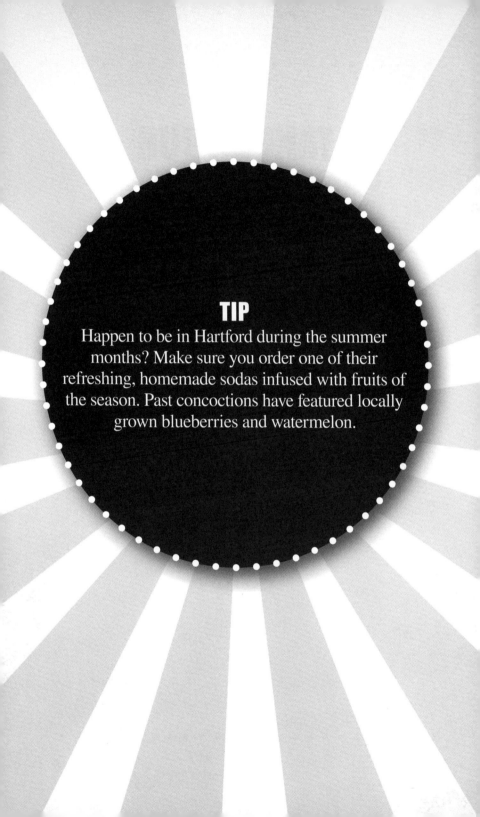

TIP

Happen to be in Hartford during the summer months? Make sure you order one of their refreshing, homemade sodas infused with fruits of the season. Past concoctions have featured locally grown blueberries and watermelon.

4

TAKE A TOUR
OF LATIN AMERICAN CUISINE IN ONE STOP

What do you get when you combine a grocery store, a shopping center, and multiple amazing restaurants all in one building? You probably get something along the lines of Hartford staple La Plaza Del Mercado, or just El Mercado for short. Featuring the most flavorful food court you'll find in these parts, El Mercado boasts restaurants featuring Mexican, Dominican, Peruvian, and Colombian fare all within mere steps of each other. It's not just the ease of having so many options in one place that makes El Mercado a go-to foodie paradise. Each option is an absolute winner, where huge portions and truly affordable prices abound, and with four very distinct and delicious styles of food at the ready, multiple trips should be planned.

704 Park St., 860-247-6449

5

EAT THAI FOOD
IN A CONVERTED LIVING ROOM

One of the most vibrant and culturally diverse streets in Hartford is Park Street. Just shy of the West Hartford line and nestled amidst the blocks of Latin, Brazilian, and Portuguese fare sits a somewhat unassuming house that actually serves up the best Thai food in town. King & I Thai Restaurant specializes in authentic Thai and Lao cuisine where everything is served fresh and spiced to perfection. The dining area sits in the "living room" of the house-turned-restaurant, lending even more of a home-cooked meal atmosphere to your dining experience. Some of the specialties that make it worth the trip include their som tum (papaya salad), fancy tofu, and pad radna dishes.

1901 Park St., 860-232-5471
kingandithaihartford.com

6

SPOIL YOUR DINNER
WITH ITALIAN COOKIES AND PASTRIES AT MOZZICATO'S

Mozzicato DePasquale Bakery and Pastry Shop is a sweet tooth heaven. Dozens of gorgeous hand-made cakes sit in the window, and inside, case upon case filled with Italian cookies and pastries beckon you to spoil your dinner in the best way possible. You simply won't find a better traditional Italian cookie anywhere else, and the almond flour cookies, especially, are to die for. Their cakes can be made to order and have adorned the tables of more weddings and special occasions than anyone can count. Cakes and cookies aren't the only things Mozzicato's specializes in. Their fresh-baked breads and homemade gelato are both highly recommended as well.

329 Franklin Ave., 860-296-0426
mozzicatobakery.com

TIP

Next door to Mozzicato's Bakery is the Mozzicato Café. Modeled after the many cafés that adorn Italian cities, they serve up a bevy of coffees, lattes, espressos, and teas. They even serve various alcoholic beverages, all while offering customers free Wi-Fi as well.

HAVE BREAKFAST OR BRUNCH
AT MO'S MIDTOWN

It might not be the biggest place in town, and its popularity sometimes leads to long wait times for tables, but the proverbial juice will be worth the squeeze. Mo's Midtown can easily lay claim to being one of the best stops anywhere for breakfast or brunch. As one Yelp user so astutely noted, "Pancakes are KING here." With a large variety to choose from, these plate-sized patties are often so flavorful you'll find yourself ignoring the maple syrup altogether. Pancakes aren't the only thing on the menu worth ordering, but whatever you do order, make sure you don't pass up that side of home fries—always delicious and seasoned to perfection.

25 Whitney St., 860-236-7741

TIP

Mo's Midtown might be great for breakfast, but they aren't for credit cards. Make sure you hit the ATM ahead of time, as they are a cash-only establishment.

GRAB A PINT
AT VAUGHAN'S PUBLIC HOUSE

There are some fantastic Irish-themed pubs all over Connecticut, and thanks to places like The Half Door and McKinnon's, Hartford residents have more than their fair share of places to choose from. But you won't find a more authentic Irish pub experience than at Vaughan's Public House. This quaint little establishment in the heart of the city is a true hidden treasure. From the handcrafted furniture that was shipped across the Atlantic from the motherland to the homemade Irish cream and signature coffees, Vaughan's brings true old-world charm to life in downtown Hartford. Go for a pint but stay for the food. Vaughan's also boasts the tastiest Irish pub menu around, highlighted by several glorious ways to prepare a potato.

59 Pratt St., 860-882-1560
irishpublichouse.com

9

EAT
AT THE POLISH NATIONAL HOME

The Polish National Home was built in 1930 to be the center for Polish–American culture and community. While they host dozens of private and public events throughout the year, what they are most known for is their award-winning cuisine. You simply won't find authentic Polish food like this anywhere else. They proudly boast that their recipes have been lovingly passed down for generations, and each meal adds credence to those claims. While they also prepare a variety of ethnic offerings, including German, French, and American meals, you'd be foolish to pass up their renowned Polish dishes. Their legendary kielbasa, pierogi, Polish rye bread, and Kapusniak (cabbage soup) are just a few of the many items considered to be must-haves.

60 Charter Oak Ave., 860-247-1784
polishhomect.org

GRAB SOME SUSHI
AT FENG

A fixture in downtown Hartford for over a decade now, Feng Asian Bistro specializes in both traditional Japanese sushi and creative Asian fusion dishes. Combining tastes from around the Pacific Rim—specifically Japanese, Chinese, and Thai—with Western flair, Feng serves up a wealth of flavors. While sushi may be the specialty (and for that reason alone you should dine here), Feng also delivers a varied menu that tempts even the most discerning palate. Their wide array of sushi, rolls, and sashimi incorporates a huge variety of flavors and culinary ingenuity. It's a beautiful, yet casual space that also includes a full bar area usually packed with locals looking to grab a bite and a drink at lunch or after work.

93 Asylum St., 860-549-3364
fengrestaurant.com

TIP

Looking to grab a quick bite to go? Try Feng's sister location, Ginza. Located right next door, Ginza specializes in delicious (and fast) to-go orders.

11

HAVE A DRINK
AT LITTLE RIVER RESTORATIVES

The relatively recent opening of Little River Restoratives served multiple purposes, not the least of which was that it reactivated a space that once held a popular local business. But it also gave Hartford residents and visitors alike a hip place to enjoy a drink where the menu was as unique and lively as the clientele. Little River Restoratives is garnering much-deserved attention for its décor and almost nightly events, but it's the array of distinctive beverages that keeps people coming back. Serving up classic cocktails, while redefining alcohol-infused punches, Little River Restoratives also offers thick beverages known as possets (White Russians and Eggnogs), and has reintroduced grogs (Tom Collins and the Gin and Tonic). One of Hartford's best watering holes for a reason.

405 Capitol Ave., 860-403-0340
lrrhartford.com

GO VEGAN (OR VEGETARIAN)
AT FIRE & SPICE

Rastafarian traditional vegetarianism has roots going back a long way. So it should not be a surprise that one of the best options in Hartford for vegan/vegetarian dishes also happens to be one of the best Jamaican restaurants around. Fire & Spice has two locations serving up organic breakfast, lunch, and dinner. While they may specialize in vegan, vegetarian, and raw food entrees, there is no lacking for flavor. Fire & Spice serves up distinctive and delicious Jamaican dishes, including such local favorites as their Jamaican jerk tofu, vegetarian Ital stew, and "Instead of Mashed Potatoes" (a blend of cauliflower, avocado, and sweet onion). You don't have to be a full-time vegetarian to enjoy Fire & Spice, but the food is so good it might make you want to.

248 Sisson Ave., 860-899-1389
491 Capitol Ave., 860-519-0476
firenspiceveganrestaurant.com

13

EAT A BIG AMOUNT
OF LITTLE DONUTS

In the Parkville section of Hartford sits an unassuming little bakery that makes possibly the best donuts you'll ever have. The best part is that you can eat a lot of them. Tastease Mini Donuts has become the stuff of legend in town. They specialize in the mini version of one of America's favorite junk foods, but don't let the size fool you. These almost bite-sized wonders pack an out-of-this-world punch. Almost as impressive as the taste is the presentation. Coming in a wide array of flavors also means a wide array of colors and designs. There are few culinary treasures as beautiful to look at (and then devour) as a full box of Tastease mini-donuts. If they are small, it means they aren't as bad for you, right?

70 New Park Ave., 860-233-2235

14

LINGER OVER TEA OR COFFEE
(OR SOMETHING ELSE) AT TISANE

Tisane Euro-Asian Café is a lot of things to a lot of people. It's a relaxing spot to enjoy one of their many unique coffees or teas for some. It's a hub of socializing where the tea-infused martinis flow and the robust menu delights for others. It's also the perfect late-night spot where the music is hot and the people are hotter. Tisane can be all of these things—and more—in just one day. The chameleon-like atmosphere is part of the charm at Tisane as the crowds shift throughout the day from those looking to unwind with a hot and/or alcoholic beverage to those looking to extend their evening until the after-midnight closing time. Either way, Tisane is one of the most welcoming spots in town.

537 Farmington Ave., 860-523-9875
mytisane.com

15

MANGIARE A SORELLA

The above would be Italian for "eat at Sorella." This is not just a recommendation; it's a warning as well. A trip to Sorella means you'll be doing a lot of eating, so go hungry because their menu is chock full of pastas, specialty dishes, and wood-fired brick oven pizza that's simply out of sight. The pizzas alone are worth the trip, as they are not only delicious but creative as well. (Avocado on pizza? It's better than you'd imagine.) Not to be outdone, their pasta and Italian specialty dishes are mouth-watering. Open for lunch and dinner, Sorella is the perfect spot when you find yourself in downtown Hartford with a hankering for something savory.

901 Main St., 860-244-9084
sorellahartford.com

TIP

Are you gluten free? You're in luck. Sorella offers gluten-free penne and dough for their pizzas. Their gluten-free pizza is one of the best in the area.

16

VISIT
SCOTTS' JAMAICAN BAKERY

For close to four decades Scotts' Jamaican Bakery has been an institution in Hartford, serving up authentic Jamaican cuisine and baking up some of the tastiest delights in the city. Their bakery serves almost a dozen different Jamaican patties, each one bursting with flavor. Throw in almost a dozen different types of Jamaican breads and some of the sweetest desserts around and you'll easily see why Scotts' is not only a cornerstone of Hartford cuisine, but why it now boasts three different locations throughout the city. Looking for a full meal? Scotts' does that too, with a variety of stews and curried dishes that will warm your heart and your belly. Large meals with a variety of sides are also available.

3381 Main St., 860-246-6599
1344 Albany Ave., 860-247-3855
630 Blue Hills Ave., 860-243-2609
scottsjamaicanbakery.com

17

SIP WINE
AT BIN228

You'll find few places in Hartford more fitting for self-proclaimed wine lovers than Bin228. With over fifty different varieties to choose from, Bin228's wine selection is both award-winning and wholly impressive. But while the wine list is a thing of beauty, it is far from the only reason to head to Bin228. The menu is packed with both comfort foods and artisan cuisine designed with true food lovers in mind. The atmosphere is exceptional as well. Exposed brick walls covered in local artwork house a European-style bistro that seems to always be filled with smiles and laughter. Bin228 is the perfect spot for both a romantic evening out and a nightcap after seeing a show.

228 Pearl St., 860-244-9463
thebin228.com

GRAB A BEER
AT CITY STEAM

Since 1997, City Steam Brewery has been in-house brewing an assortment of frosty beverages using a unique brewing process that utilizes city-provided steam, hence the name. (Be sure to ask someone behind the bar about the process. They'll tell you all about it.) The highly recognizable City Steam line of beer can be found all over the state of Connecticut and beyond, but there is really nothing like trying out their "Naughty Nurse" or a "Blonde on Blonde" inside the stunning, nine-level brownstone that houses the operations. Not to be out done by the brewmaster, the kitchen crew serves up a large menu featuring such specialties as all-day omelets, char-broiled burgers, and stone-baked pizzas.

942 Main St., 860-525-1600
citysteam.biz

TIP

Looking to laugh out loud? City Steam is also home to the Brew HaHa Comedy Club, which regularly hosts professional comedians from all over the world.

FILL UP
AT BEAR'S SMOKEHOUSE

What's a transplant from Kansas City to do in Hartford? Open a barbecue joint, of course. Making their goal to serve up the best Kansas City–style barbecue this side of the Mississippi, Bear's Smokehouse BBQ instantly became a go-to spot for meat lovers in Hartford. Using their own unique techniques and recipes, complete with homemade rubs and sauces, Bear's owners have put themselves on the map for serving up some of the best barbeque around. Don't just take our word for it. Their high marks from both the *New York Times* and various reputable, local reviewers should tell you all you need to know. Bear's also offers a to-go menu of sliced meat by the pound, so if you can't stay for a meal, you can take some home with you for later.

89 Arch St., 860-785-8772
bearsbbq.com

PLAN A WEEK
OF MEXICAN EATS

From a culinary standpoint, there are a lot of things Hartford does well. One thing the city really excels at, though, is Mexican food. Everyone knows the best Mexican food comes from little mom-and-pop locales, and Hartford has some of the best. Each one has its own style of authentic Mexican cuisine, and each one has its own specialties as well. Many locals consider these to be the top three Mexican restaurants in town (in alphabetical order):

Coyote Flaco
635 New Britain Ave., 860-953-1299
coyoteflacohartford.com

El Nuevo Serape Restaurant
931 Broad St., #1, 860-547-1884
elnuevosarape.com

Monte Albán
531 Farmington Ave., 860-523-7423
montealbanhartford.com

STOCK UP
ON PASTA AT DIFIORE

There are quite a few musts when talking about Hartford's Little Italy section centered on Franklin Avenue, not the least of which is Difiore Ravioli Shop. This independently owned pasta shop has been supplying area residents with some of the best homemade pastas and sauces around for three generations. The fact that they have ravioli in the restaurant name should tip you off to just one of their many specialties. Go for the ravioli, but go home with as many things as you can carry. With a dozen pasta varieties and close to twenty sauces to choose from, you could have a different amazing Italian dish, fresh from their kitchen to yours, for as many nights running as your heart desires.

556 Franklin Ave., 860-296-1077
difioreraviolishop.com

HAVE A BEER AT THE SPIGOT

Some places attract customers with frills and gimmicks but the Spigot Cafe has continued to deliver a satisfying experience for over fifty years strong, with no frills or gimmicks attached. This Hartford watering hole is a perennial favorite in local "Best Of" voting, but it's solely because of its great beer selection, laid-back atmosphere, and some of the friendliest conversation to be found in Hartford. The Spigot has a massive selection of beers, whiskeys, and bourbons to choose from, so discerning drinkers are sure to find something they love. Best of all, the Spigot lets you bring in your own food so you can combine all your favorites into one night out.

468 Prospect Ave., 860-236-7663
hartford.com/spigot

23

VISIT THE SPANISH COASTLINE

VIA COSTA DEL SOL

Galicia, in northwestern Spain, is famous for its wine and exotic seafood dishes, both of which you will find done with equal parts tradition and distinction, at Costa del Sol. It is the perfect place for anyone looking for some of the tastiest delights the Mediterranean region has to offer. Costa del Sol also specializes in tapas dishes, so those looking for a light bite while experimenting with the wine selection are in luck. This warm and friendly restaurant offers beautiful décor and an outdoor patio that is the perfect spot for a night out with friends or family.

901 Wethersfield Ave., 860-296-1714
costadelsolhartford.com

ATTEND
A KNOW GOOD MARKET

Designed as a community-building event that aims to draw together people from virtually all walks of life, the Know Good Market is the perfect place to grab a bite and maybe make some new friends in the process. Held the second Thursday of the month from May through October, the Know Good Market includes specialty food trucks from all over the state, as well as from local restaurants. This unique dining destination also includes live music, and in the summer months you can shop for fresh, locally grown produce courtesy of Knox, Inc., a local horticulture hub. The Market events run during the early evening, and entry into these open-air street fests is free and open to the public. So go hungry and leave happy.

30-50 Bartholomew Ave.
breakfastxlunchxdinner.com/kgm

25

EXPERIENCE

A MEAL AT ON20

If haute cuisine in an elegant setting is your speed, then On20 should probably be the first stop you make when dining in Hartford. Featuring award-winning contemporary American cuisine sourced from local ingredients, On20 has been recognized as one of the top restaurants in the country by Opentable.com and others. Their seasonal menu consistently offers a supreme fine dining experience. On20 is situated on the twentieth floor of the Hartford Steam Boiler Building and offers breathtaking views of both downtown Hartford and the Connecticut River. There is truly not a bad seat in the house when it comes to the view and not a bad choice to make when it comes to the menu. Needless to say, it's the perfect spot for a romantic night out as well.

1 State St., 20th Floor, 860-722-5161
ontwenty.com

26

EXPERIENCE
A TASTE OF PERU AT PIOLIN

For those who want to experience—or already love—Peruvian cuisine, Hartford has what you need in the form of Piolin Restaurant. So popular they had to open a second location, Piolin is by far the most authentic Peruvian restaurant anywhere in the area. Piolin offers a truly stellar selection of traditional Peruvian dishes, including multiple styles of lomo saltado (beef strips), tallarin (a pasta dish), chaufa (fried rice), a huge seafood selection, and so much more. Their menu runs impressively deep with variety—soups, salads, seafood, grilled specialties, and a "Peruvian Style" section that really showcases the traditional flavors of Peru.

417 New Britain Ave., 860-293-1255
395 Franklin Ave., 860-296-2062
piolin2.com

TAKE A TOUR
OF HARTFORD FLAVOR COMPANY

The Hartford Flavor Company's mission is to provide uniquely flavored liqueurs and to make the creative cocktail an essential part of the social and dining experience. They are off to a great start. Their Wild Moon Liqueurs come in a variety of unique flavors (Cucumber? Chai Spice?) and have recently been cited as a "healthy" alcohol choice thanks to their additive- and GMO-free recipes. Every Friday, Saturday, and Sunday you can visit Diana's Lair, the tasting room and full bar located in their historic manufacturing building. The nominal entry fee to Diana's Lair gets you a tour of the production process, tastings of current Wild Moon flavors, cocktail samples, and appetizers offered from some of the better local restaurants.

30 Arbor St., 860-338-1642
hartfordflavor.com

28

EXPERIENCE

A TASTE OF COLOMBIA AT LA FONDA

Needless to say, quite a few international cuisines are represented in Hartford. La Fonda brings traditional Colombian cooking to Hartford's south end. This cuisine includes such specialties as an impressive lineup of arepa (stuffed cornbread) dishes and various offerings revolving around plantains. What La Fonda might be most known for, though, are their empanadas. For some, these little beef or chicken pastry turnovers may be a perfect appetizer, but others might wish to order them as a main meal. Tuesday through Friday, La Fonda runs a lunch special where the helpings are huge and the prices affordable. Pop in on Thursday nights and you can get your karaoke fix as well.

269 Franklin Ave., 860-296-8256
lafondahartford.com

29

GRAB A DOG
AT WOODY'S

Woody's is nothing short of a Hartford institution. It's known for being featured on an episode of the hit TV show *Man Vs. Food* and for having a Miami Dolphins-friendly bar attached to the restaurant, just for starters. But what they are really known for are their hot dogs. Woody's has a varied menu featuring specialty hot dogs you'll only find here. Woody's delights in putting fun and creative spins on the traditional hot dog. If you can slather it on a dog, Woody's probably has it on their menu. Baked beans, coleslaw, bacon, pulled pork, and even mac & cheese find their way onto some of Woody's dogs.

915 Main St., 860-278-5499
woodyshotdog.com

30

GET A QUICK BITE
AT ONE OF THE KITCHENS

The Billings Forge Community Works has been using food to build community and change the lives of local residents for quite some time now. They run a year-round farmers market and a community garden that supplies food to their cafés and catering business. The Kitchen at Billings Forge and its sister location inside Hartford Public Library offer a delicious café-style menu featuring a variety of salads and sandwiches. They also have a small breakfast menu and serve up fresh-baked desserts as well. Both the Kitchen at Billings Forge and the Kitchen at Hartford Public Library are the perfect pit stop for breakfast or lunch on the go, while also supporting a great cause.

The Kitchen at Billings Forge
559 Broad St., 860-727-8066
billingsforgeworks.org/the-kitchen-billings-forge

The Kitchen at Hartford Public Library
500 Main St., 860-695-6300

MAKE A STOP
AT THE FIRST & LAST TAVERN

Established in 1936, First & Last Tavern has been filling bellies in the south end of Hartford for just about as long as anyone can remember. Named for being the last stop before heading outside Hartford city limits, and the first when crossing back over the line, First & Last Tavern has a rich history behind that tasty Italian menu. Specializing in coal-fired brick oven pizzas and a pasta sauce that everyone loves, First & Last Tavern has been reeling in the culinary awards for quite some time. Wish you could just jar that pasta sauce and take it with you? You can, for yourself or in a gift box of sauces. This is down home Italian cooking with a friendly, family-like atmosphere.

939 Maple Ave., 860-956-6000
firstandlasttavern.com

TIP

Right across the street sits the First & Last Bakery, serving up a heavenly variety of freshly baked pastries. They also have a full café menu serving breakfast and lunch.

GRAB A GRINDER
FROM FRANKLIN GIANT SANDWICH SHOP

If you've never been to New England, you've probably never heard the term "grinder" before; perhaps you call them heroes, subs, or hoagies. Regardless of what you call them, the biggest and best ones in Hartford are at Franklin Giant Sandwich Shop. When you've got "giant" in your name, the sandwiches had better live up to the hype, and in this case they absolutely do. Massive sandwiches packed with whatever meats, cheeses, and veggies you want are this shop's forte. While the locals sing the praises of their pizza, it's the massive grinders that make it worth the trip.

464 Franklin Ave., 860-296-6574
franklingiantsandwichct.com

EXPERIENCE ETHIOPIAN CUISINE

AT ABYSSINIAN

In Hartford West End there sits an unassuming spot that serves up some of the more distinct and flavorful cuisine the city has to offer. Abyssinian Ethiopian Restaurant offers authentic, home-style Ethiopian cuisine in a modest and warm environment. In true Ethiopian fashion, meals are served on a light, crepe-style flatbread (injera) that serves as your only utensil. This hands-on style of dining adds to the cultural experience that's punctuated by a range of truly succulent dishes. With a menu that features chicken, beef, lamb, fish, and vegetarian dishes, Abyssinian has something for everyone. Fans of lentils will consider this place next to heaven thanks to the abundance of the tasty legume in various dishes.

533 Farmington Ave., 860-218-2231
abyssinianethiopian.com

34

STOP BY
THE HANGING HILLS TASTING ROOM

One of the newest additions to the rich craft beer history of Hartford is Hanging Hills Brewing Company. Utilizing locally sourced ingredients and with an eye toward both environmental responsibility and community building, Hanging Hills is delicious beer with a conscience. On weekends and Thursday and Friday evenings, you can visit their tasting room where pints and to-go growlers are available. This quaint watering hole with the hand-crafted bar offers an extensive tap list featuring all of Hanging Hills' most popular beers. An equally extensive list of growlers is on sale for a reasonable price as well. You can bring your own growler to fill, but make sure you read up on the growler policy on their website before you go.

150 Ledyard St., 860-263-7033
hanginghillsbrewery.com

SPEND AN EVENING
AT THE RUSSELL

Located in the heart of downtown Hartford, the Russell is the perfect space to spend a relaxing evening, especially if you are attending an event or conference at the XL Center across the street. The Russell is a multilevel space serving lunch and dinner, but also includes a full service bar. With warm décor styled after classic island hotels, the Russell works for both an intimate evening out or a social gathering. Their lower level consists of the first floor bar and patio seating for dinner guests. There's also the Red Room Lounge used for dining as well. The second-level mezzanine is an added bonus for those looking to combine a cocktail with great conversation.

103 Pratt St., 860-727-4014
therussellct.com

PURCHASE SOME SAUSAGE
FROM LAROSA'S

LaRosa's Marketplace has been a family-owned and -operated business since the 1930s. Their specialty is sausage, but not just any sausage. LaRosa's specializes in homemade, fresh-every-day sausage free of the fillers and preservatives you find in your local grocery stores. Their sausages come in sweet, medium, and hot varieties, and the selection includes flavors as varied as sundried tomato, barbecue, and basil and cheese, among others. It's the perfect, mouth-watering addition to pretty much any meal. At LaRosa's you go for the sausage, but you can take home an entire meal as well. This rustic Italian deli also serves weekly specials that include soups, salads, signature wraps, grinders, and even breakfast sandwiches.

94 Brown St., 860-296-1909
larosamarketplace.com

HAVE BRUNCH
AT THE PLACE 2 BE

This recently re-opened spot in the South End section of Hartford offers an impressive breakfast and lunch menu seven days a week. The space itself is huge, spotless, and accommodating to larger parties. The atmosphere and service are welcoming and the food is always top notch. The Place 2 Be has a diverse menu, especially on the lunch side. Greek-themed dishes like gyros, souvlaki, and several different pita flatbread dishes complement burgers, clubs, and grinders. No matter what you get for a meal, make sure you save room for a milkshake. These beautifully decorated milkshakes, with names like Vanilla Birthday Cake and Chocoholic Cannoli, are pure decadence. Hands down the best milkshake you'll find that isn't from an ice cream shop.

615 Franklin Ave., 860-904-7891
place2bect.com

GET IN THE BUFFET LINE
AT BRAZIL GRILL

Brazil Grill will change your mind about how you view buffet-style food. At Brazil Grill the buffet tables are laden with authentic Brazilian cuisine, including an assortment of rice, veggies, fruits, and other sides. But it's the meat-carving station that keeps people coming back for more. These churrasco-style meats are seasoned to perfection, then slow roasted on a rotisserie until tender . Brazil Grill is a casual, simple place where the food is always fresh and the atmosphere welcoming. There's ample reason why this is continually rated one of the best Brazilian spots in the state.

1996 Park St., 860-523-5477

SPEND AN EVENING
AT CASONA

On Casona's website they call themselves "The Music Lounge" and ask patrons to eat, drink, and be merry. This is great advice that is easy to follow at this upbeat restaurant. You'll certainly eat well, as Casona offers a vast menu of Latin American and Caribbean fare that proudly features cuisines from seven different countries. Their signature drink menu also has a Latin/Caribbean flair but features several martini, beer, and wine options as well. Finally, it's hard not to be merry when there are two rooms of music. While one room focuses on Top 40 and DJ nights, the other is strictly for Latin music, including salsa, merengue, and Latin jazz. Casona even offers free salsa lessons for beginners on Fridays and Saturdays.

681 Wethersfield Ave., 860-578-8416
casonahartfordct.com

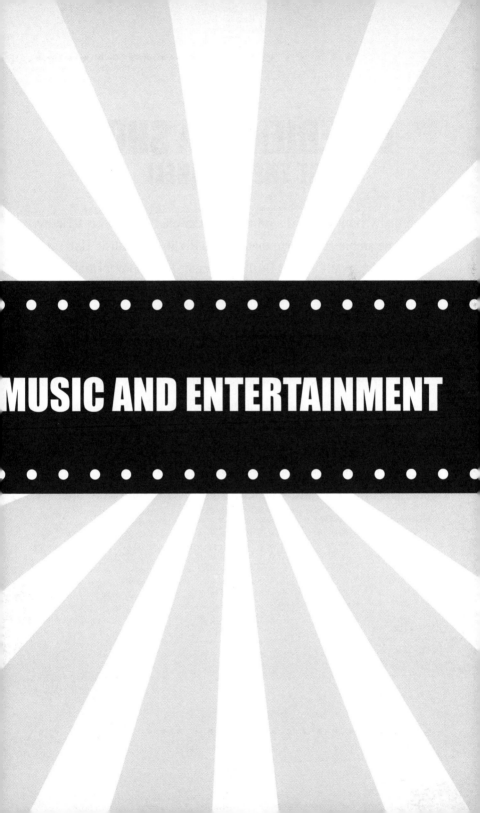

MUSIC AND ENTERTAINMENT

EXPERIENCE A SHOW
AT THE BUSHNELL

Originally built in 1930, and designed in classic art deco style by the same architectural firm that created Radio City Music Hall (and built two years prior), the Bushnell Center for the Performing Arts is a gorgeous venue with a rich history in the performing arts. Now composed of the original twenty-seven-hundred-seat Mortensen Hall and the nine-hundred-seat Belding Theater, the Bushnell offers an annual series of Broadway production, and has hosted major performers from the worlds of music, comedy, spoken word, and more. On any given night at the Bushnell you can take in a ballet, hear the Hartford Symphony Orchestra, or enjoy an evening of stories delivered by A-list celebrities. Dubbed a "Connecticut cultural treasure" by Connecticut Public Television, the Bushnell continues to be a must-see destination over eighty years after its doors first opened.

166 Capitol Ave., 860-987-6000
bushnell.org

IMMERSE YOURSELF
IN IMPROV

As stand-up comedy once again became relevant and comedy clubs began to pop up all over the country, one group of Hartford residents took it to the next level and formed one of the most successful and celebrated improv troupes on the East Coast. Sea Tea Improv is a veritable tour de force, with live programming and workshops available almost every night. But it's not just the quantity that's impressive to behold, the quality is top-notch as well. Their new Sea Tea Comedy Theater is an intimate space where the laughs flow like wine and just like that proverbial box of chocolates, you never know what you're going to get. Such is the beauty of improv on a live stage. The unpredictability of it all is half the fun.

15 Asylum St., 860-578-4832
seateaimprov.com

42

MAKE MONDAYS FUN
WITH FREE JAZZ IN THE PARK

Produced by the Hartford Jazz Society, Monday Night Jazz is the nation's longest-running free jazz concert series. Taking place over the course of six weeks in July and August, this Hartford staple will be celebrating its 50th anniversary in 2017. Every Monday while the weather is getting warmer, Bushnell Park is heating up with some of the hottest jazz acts from all over the country. The laid-back, family-friendly vibe at the Monday Night Jazz concerts gives the whole thing a festival-like atmosphere (minus the overpriced drinks and drunken debauchery). Pack yourself a picnic dinner or partake in a delicacy from one of the ever-present food trucks. Either way, bring a blanket and be prepared to be lulled into summer bliss by some of the smoothest sounds around.

Bushnell Park, 860-242-6688
hartfordmondaynightjazz.com

43

VISIT
THE CHARTER OAK CULTURAL CENTER

The Charter Oak Cultural Center is a nonprofit arts exhibition and performance space that is housed in the building that served as Connecticut's first synagogue, built in 1876. Today, Charter Oak Cultural Center is a haven for multicultural arts of all disciplines and a bastion for exploring the burning issues in our current society. Their programming includes everything from art installations and live music to documentary screenings and various readings. It's an eclectic mix of events that incorporates many of the peoples and cultures that permeate the very fabric of Hartford society. Not to mention that the space itself is as beautiful as you would expect a former house of worship built in the 19th century to be.

21 Charter Oak Ave., 860-310-2580
charteroakcenter.org

44

SEE A SHOW
AT HARTFORD STAGE

When a theater is under the artistic direction of a two-time Tony Award winner, you would be safe in expecting big and bold things to take place on its stage. For the award-winning Hartford Stage, its national reputation as one of the best regional theaters in the country is well-earned. Hartford Stage is known for producing innovative revivals and boundary-pushing new plays alike, often giving audiences a first look at productions that eventually find their way to Broadway and/or travelling the world over. Their recent takes on the works of Shakespeare have been must-see theater, even for those who hated the Bard in high school. Meanwhile, their cavalcade of thought-provoking works tackling contemporary issues leaves no societal stones unturned.

50 Church St., 860-527-5151
hartfordstage.org

SEE A SHOW
AT THEATERWORKS, TOO

Not to be outdone by their neighbors across town, Hartford's TheaterWorks produces engaging contemporary theater in a space housed in the historic City Arts on Pearl building (built in 1927). Originally founded in 1985, TheaterWorks has produced over 130 plays, including multiple world premieres and Pulitzer Prize winners. TheaterWorks' intimate space has allowed patrons to get up close and personal with the performers, which recently included Academy Award winner Richard Dreyfus playing the role of Albert Einstein. Their goal is to constantly provide unique insights into the human experience, so TheaterWorks performances are often as powerful as they are touching. With a season that often runs eleven months out of the year, there are plenty of opportunities to have a moving experience at TheaterWorks.

233 Pearl St., 860-527-7838
theaterworkshartford.org

GET THE BLUES
AT BLACK-EYED SALLY'S

Just about every night of the week the soulful sounds that have defined American music can be heard at Black-Eyed Sally's. Sally's is a world-renowned, award-winning music venue that specializes in blues, jazz, roots music, and good old-fashioned rock 'n' roll. This longtime fixture of the national blues circuit has expanded its repertoire over the years to include a more diverse musical lineup, but there's still nothing like diving into a big plate of their succulent BBQ while some Chicago-style blues band tears it up on stage. Oh, did we forget to mention that Black-Eyed Sally's is also an award-winning BBQ joint? You can feed your stomach, your ears, and your soul all in one shot at Sally's.

350 Asylum St., 860-278-7427
blackeyedsallys.com

ACQUIRE A NEW APPRECIATION FOR OPERA

Long ago, opera was a genre for the masses. It wasn't until somewhat recently that opera became a chosen art form for the upper crust. The Hartford Opera Theater is on a mission to bring opera back to the masses, one innovative production at a time. Offering quality opera productions at affordable prices is a feat in and of itself, but offering opera productions that are also culturally and topically relevant is equally impressive. Somehow Hartford Opera Theater manages to pull it off with aplomb. Their tagline is "Opera for Everyone," and that couldn't be more true. With productions that are often family-friendly (and sans any sort of strict dress code), Hartford Opera Theater provides the perfect opportunity to further explore or introduce yourself to the operatic genre.

860-578-4393
hartfordoperatheater.com

HEED THE CALL
OF THE PIPES

Danny Boy is not the only one the pipes are calling for. For one Saturday every September, Mortensen's Riverfront Plaza goes green, and not just from recycling. The annual "Pipes in the Valley" is the region's largest Celtic Music Festival, bringing in acts not only from all over the United States but from the motherlands as well. Over the course of an entire day, the riverfront area is filled with the sights and sounds of Celtic music like you've never experienced before. It's a rousing (and free) affair that also features step dancing, sword demonstrations, various athletic games, Celtic food and drink, loads of child-friendly activities, and of course bagpipes.

300 Columbus Blvd.
pipesinthevalley.com

49

ENJOY THE MUSIC
AT INFINITY HALL

Out in the northwest corner of the state, Infinity Hall has established quite a following with an array of musical talent, both national and local, that comes across its stage. Thankfully now for folks in the greater Hartford area, the drive isn't quite as long. Infinity Music Hall & Bistro opened a second, larger location in downtown Hartford to much fanfare, and they've kept up their end of the bargain by delivering one of the best listening experiences around. The acoustics and stellar sound system greatly enhance the trip to Infinity Hall for the quality acts they host (which includes Grammy-winners and world-renowned talents). The ability to grab a meal and a drink at their in-house bistro is a definite bonus.

32 Front St., 860-560-7757
infinityhall.com

EXPERIENCE
A TNMOT AZTRO PERFORMANCE

There are dance troupes, there is performance art, and then there is TNMoT AZTRo. Seamlessly blending a diverse group of visual mediums with dance, this Hartford-based company is helping to redefine how art is expressed through original and thought-provoking pieces. Fashion, film, music, visual arts, and, of course, dance all come together in swirls of sight and sound that will not only entertain but, quite often, amaze. TNMoT AZTRo pieces have been performed at a variety of locations throughout the city, including the Wadsworth Atheneum, Real Art Ways, and the Town and Country Club. The elaborate nature of their productions means that TNMoT AZTRo events aren't done on any regular schedule, but their website and Facebook page have upcoming performance info.

860-680-5348
tnmotaztro.com

ATTEND
A HARTFORD SYMPHONY ORCHESTRA PERFORMANCE

Since their humble beginnings in 1934, the Hartford Symphony Orchestra has spent decades enriching the lives of area residents and bringing high-quality musical performances to the masses. The Hartford Symphony Orchestra holds the majority of their performances in the stunning Belding and Mortensen Halls at the Bushnell Performing Arts Center. But they've also been known to entertain audiences with stripped down performances such as their popular "Sunday Serenades" chamber music series at the Wadsworth Atheneum. Showcasing everything from the masters of Classical music to popular film scores and symphonic takes on pop music, the Symphony is the epitome of musical excellence with a little something for everyone to enjoy.

166 Capitol Ave., 860-987-5900
hartfordsymphony.org

ATTEND
THE GREATER HARTFORD FESTIVAL OF JAZZ

While Monday nights in the heat of summer belong to local jazz fans, the crown jewel for all true jazz aficionados in the area is the Greater Hartford Festival of Jazz. Originally begun in 1992, this free festival has grown into the largest free jazz event in all of New England. It's been estimated that as many as 70,000 of your closest friends visited Bushnell Park for the 2016 edition of this multi-day festival. Usually held in mid-July, Jazz Fest (as it's known by the locals) is truly one of the highlights of Hartford's musical calendar, bringing in dozens of world-renowned musicians. Jazz Fest is also the perfect excursion for a family night out and features food and other types of vendors galore.

Bushnell Park
hartfordjazz.org

SEE A FILM
AT CINESTUDIO

The beautiful campus of Trinity College is home to a film buff's haven. Originally formed by a collective of Trinity students in 1970, Cinestudio has been delivering the absolute best in groundbreaking cinema for over four decades. From cult classics to foreign films to controversial new productions that mainstream theaters won't touch, Cinestudio is truly a home away from home for cinephiles. Housed in an old lecture hall that was originally built in 1935, and refurbished to replicate a 1930s film house, Cinestudio may also be the most aesthetically pleasing venue in which to see a movie. Throw in their top-notch sound and projection systems, and this single-screen venue offers a complete experience, not just a movie. Grab a balcony seat (if you can) for maximum viewing pleasure.

300 Summit St., 860-297-2463
cinestudio.org

EXPERIENCE A SHOW
AT HARTBEAT ENSEMBLE

If you're looking for an intimate spot to see provocative theater, then look no further than HartBeat Ensemble. The plays produced at HartBeat Ensemble are original, full-length works that focus on "extraordinary stories of ordinary people." The goal of HartBeat Ensemble is to present theater to the community while breaking down our traditionally held concepts of class, gender, and race. While it's theater with a purpose, it's also theater that extends to all genres, from comedy to realism and beyond. With a recent move into their own Carriage House Theater, HartBeat Ensemble is able to offer a full season of events and productions in a cozy space where the members of the audience often feel like they are part of the action.

360 Farmington Ave., 860-548-9144
hartbeatensemble.org

ATTEND A PERFORMANCE
AT THE ACADEMY OF THE ARTS

Hartford has its fair share of professional and community theater, but there are some impressive youngsters doing their thing as well. The Greater Hartford Academy of the Arts is a multidiscipline arts high school that brings in students from all over Connecticut and is consistently recognized on a national level. Offering courses of study from creative writing and visual arts to music, dance, and various forms of theater, the Academy also produces multiple performances that are open to the general public. Utilizing either the six-hundred-seat theater or the smaller "black box" performance space, students annually produce and perform everything from full-scale musicals to intimate theatrical productions. Each and every performance is a showcase for some truly talented individuals, both on stage and behind the scenes.

359 Washington St., 860-757-6388
crecschools.org/our-schools/greater-hartford-academy-of-the-arts

56

CHILL
AT THE BLACK-EYED & BLUES FEST

Annually for the past seventeen years, Hartford's Bushnell Park is transformed into a blues-lover's haven for one Saturday in June. Thanks to those purveyors of all things blues at Black-Eyed Sally's, the Black-Eyed & Blues Fest has become a Hartford tradition and a staple of the local summertime festival circuit. Usually kicking off around mid-afternoon and rolling deep into the summer evening, the Black-Eyed & Blues Fest is a family-friendly affair that also showcases multiple food tents (including, of course, Black-Eyed Sally's famous barbeque) serving up delicious eats and craft beers. The Black-Eyed & Blues Fest is always free admission and open to the general public. Be sure to get there early and plan to stay late, because the musical lineup is usually pretty stellar.

Bushnell Park, 860-278-7427
blackeyedsallys.com

HIT UP
A COMIC-CON, OR TWO

Even if you are not a comic book, video game, or cosplay fan, you should be aware of the "cons" popping up all over the country. Hartford is lucky enough to have not one but two comic-cons call it home. The ConnectiCon takes place every July at the Connecticut Convention Center, whereas the Hartford ComiConn takes place in September at the XL Center in downtown Hartford. Featuring loads of celebrity appearances, panels, workshops, gaming consoles, tabletop games, and exhibitors of all kinds, both events make for a fun-filled romp through the gaming, comic, and role-playing worlds. But you don't really have to be involved with any of those scenes to enjoy these events. The costume watching alone is worth the price of admission.

ConnectiCon
connecticon.org

Hartford ComiConn
comiconn.com

58

ATTEND
A HARTT SCHOOL PERFORMANCE

The Hartt School is an internationally recognized performing arts conservatory at the University of Hartford. The Hartt School offers multiple programs in music, dance, and theater, and you get the chance to witness the fruits of their labor. The Hartt School utilizes several performance spaces housed in three buildings on the University of Hartford campus that range from super intimate to a 750-seat theater. Performances include full musical theater productions, symphonies, concertos, jazz recitals, and various styles of dance, among others. The Hartt School facilities also host a wide array of outside performers from both around the region and well beyond. Can't make it to a performance in person? You might be in luck, because the Hartt School also live streams a handful of them.

200 Bloomfield Ave., 860-768-4228
hartford.edu/hartt

HANG OUT
AT SULLY'S PUB

When a lot of other venues in Hartford started to move towardbooking only cover bands, there were a handful that stood strong behind local, original music. One of those venues was Sully's Pub. Ask anyone where to find hip-hop in Hartford, and they will probably point you to Sully's. But Sully's welcomes all types of music to their two stages. When the weather is warm and the sun is shining, you'll find bands playing in their outdoor tiki bar. Year-round their indoor stage is alive with music. From hip-hop to reggae to punk rock and everything in between, Sully's has become one of the more welcoming music venues in all of Hartford.

2071 Park St., 860-231-8881
sullyspub.com

TIP

You can make a night of it at Sully's without ever leaving the building. Housed in the conjoining building next door is Lena's First & Last Pizza, serving up gourmet pizzas and other Italian fare.

60

EXPERIENCE
THE TRINITY INTERNATIONAL HIP-HOP FESTIVAL

Every spring for over a decade now, Trinity College, in the heart of Hartford, has hosted a festival bent on uniting different communities through hip-hop. The Trinity International Hip-Hop Festival has grown into one of the most unique and acclaimed music events the city has to offer. The use of the term "international" in the title isn't just hyperbole either. This event has brought in hip-hop artists from over fifty different countries. It continually combines local and regional artists with artists from almost every continent and hip-hop legends such as KRS One. The festival is a socially conscious one, often with themes revolving around unity through hip-hop music and culture. It also features panel discussions and a one-day youth conference sponsored by the city.

300 Summit St.
trinityhiphop.com

ATTEND
A FILM FESTIVAL, OR TWO

Fans of cutting-edge socially conscious independent film, rejoice. You may have just found your home away from home in Hartford. The city is host to more than its fair share of annual film festivals, many of which are culturally or socially themed. Some selections to choose from:

Hartford Jewish Film Festival
hjff.org

Out Film CT–Connecticut's LGBT Film Festival
outfilmct.org

Trinity Film Festival
trinityfilmfestival.org

Reel Youth Hartford Film Festival
reelyouthhartford.org

NIGHT
FALL

62

CELEBRATE
HARTFORD AND A HOOKER

Hartford.com's annual Hooker Day Parade honors Hartford's founder, Thomas Hooker. This family-friendly parade is a Mardi Gras–style event complete with extravagant costumes, giant puppets, brass bands, and just about anything else you can think of that would turn a parade into a party. After years of being just a parade, Hooker Day is now an all-encompassing event that finishes up in Bushnell Park, with a beer garden, food trucks, a makers market, and musical entertainment, among other things. Hooker Day is a celebration of all things Hartford and is centered on celebrating the creativity of its people. The parade is open to anyone and everyone, though some sort of costume is required to be included in the march.

hartford.com/hookerday

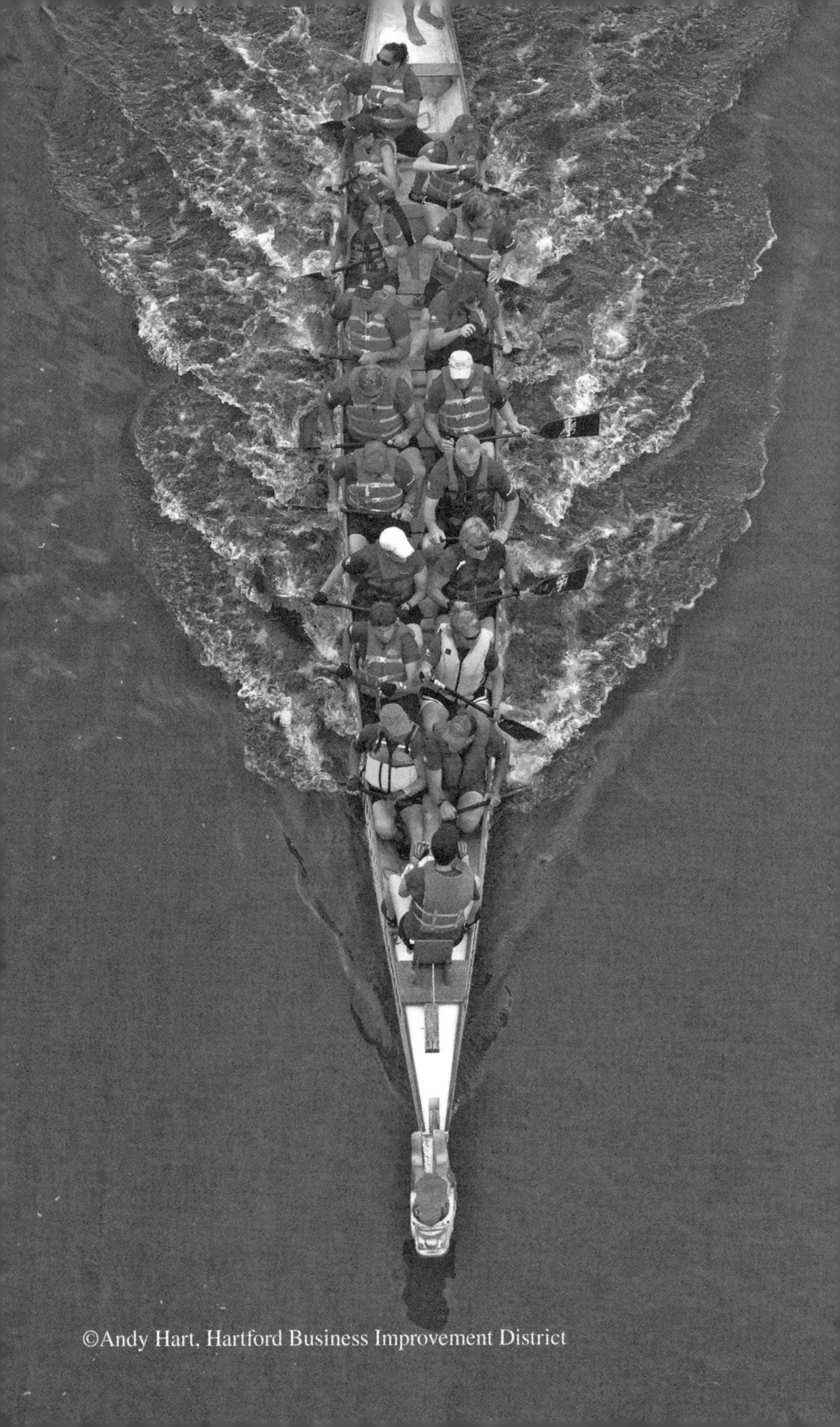

SPORTS AND RECREATION

63

RACE
IN THE ART SLED DERBY

Every February, just when even winter's biggest fans start to long for the warmth of spring, a group of people gather on a hill in Elizabeth Park and transform a normal, chilly Saturday into one of the best parts of the season. The Hartford Art Sled Derby is unlike any other wintertime event in Hartford. These homemade sleds really must be seen to be believed. Giant pirate ships, sleds built to look like Star Wars vehicles, a guy in a shark suit riding in a shark-shaped sled—you name it, this derby has it. Everyone is welcome to build their own dream sled and send it careening down the hill. For the slightly less adventurous, just attending and watching the madness is more than enough fun.

Elizabeth Park Overlook
facebook.com/Hartford-Art-Sled-Derby-1546597145576882/

ICE SKATE
IN BUSHNELL PARK DURING WINTERFEST

Beginning at the end of November and continuing through the holidays into January, Bushnell Park in downtown Hartford is transformed into a winter wonderland. Winterfest Hartford is an annual celebration of all things frosty and festive, complete with free photos with Santa and holiday-themed programming. But the centerpiece to Winterfest is the outdoor ice skating rink. Free and open to the public, the rink has become one of the biggest treats for kids of all ages in the greater Hartford area. Ice skating novices are welcome too, as the rink staff offer free lessons. There's nothing quite like gliding across the ice on a brisk winter evening while the lights and the sounds of laughter surround you. It's like a Norman Rockwell painting come to life.

Bushnell Park
theiquiltplan.org/initiatives/winterfest

Do
Not
Step
On
The
Legs

RIDE
THE BUSHNELL PARK CAROUSEL

It's not often you'll find a working vintage wooden carousel in the heart of a city. But nestled inside the downtown oasis that is Bushnell Park is the Bushnell Park Carousel, a fully functioning carousel originally built in 1914. Relocated to Hartford from Ohio in the mid-70s, the Bushnell Park Carousel has been a main attraction of downtown Hartford for children and adults alike. For only $1 per ride, you can whirl your worries away on gorgeously decorated, hand-carved wooden horses while the booming Wurlitzer organ plays a wide selection of carnival and pop culture tunes. It's a three-minute step back in time to when entertainment value wasn't tied to an electronic device or Internet connection.

1 Jewell St., 860-585-5411
facebook.com/bushnellparkcarousel

SPEND THE DAY
IN ELIZABETH PARK

Located right on the line between Hartford and West Hartford, Elizabeth Park is one of the most beautiful locations in the area. The park covers 102 acres and is renowned for its amazing rose garden, semi-hidden pathways, scenic pond, greenhouses, and an assortment of courts—tennis, basketball, lawn bowling, and more. Picnickers and photographers are not only welcomed, but also encouraged. In addition, Elizabeth Park plays host to a plethora of special events throughout the year, including a summer concert series, outdoor yoga lessons, and free outdoor movies, just to name a few. Don't feel like bringing your own lunch? No worries. The park also features the award-winning Pond House Café. They even have a take-out window during the summer months specializing in gourmet hot dogs and ice cream.

1561 Asylum Ave., 860-231-9443
elizabethparkct.org

67

CRUISE
ALONG THE CONNECTICUT RIVER

Hartford's Mortensen Riverfront Plaza and Charter Oak Landing both serve as departure points for two different Connecticut River cruise lines. From just prior to Memorial Day weekend to about mid-October, the forty-nine-passenger *Hartford Belle* takes sightseers on sixty- and ninety-minute cruises that feature ample seating, gorgeous views, a full bar, and light snacks. It can be quite majestic travelling up and down sections of New England's longest river on a beautiful summer afternoon. The *Hartford Belle* runs on weekends, with additional weekday hours in July and August. Hartford also happens to be one of the stops for some of the themed Lady Katherine Cruises that originate out of nearby Middletown. You'll get a new appreciation for Hartford and the surrounding area by seeing it from the water.

860-665-9428
hartfordbelle.com

866-867-4837
ladykatherinecruises.com

68

CHEER ON THE HUSKIES

AT A UCONN BASKETBALL GAME

What Hartford lacks in professional sports teams, the city more than makes up for in collegiate sports. When you think college basketball, especially women's college basketball, most schools pale in comparison to the University of Connecticut. For both men's and women's squads, their home away from home is the XL Center in downtown Hartford. Each year area residents are treated to multiple games from both teams. When the XL Center is filled with thousands of raucous UConn fans, these games have an almost NBA-type energy and excitement to them. It doesn't hurt that the women's team is currently on a four-year run as national champs, and the men's team frequently qualifies for the NCAA Tournament.

225 Trumbull St., 860-249-6333
xlcenter.com

69

ATTEND
A WOLF PACK GAME

Anyone who knows Hartford knows that Hartford loves its hockey. The Hartford Whalers left town in 1997, yet Whalers merchandise still sells better than any other noncurrent NHL team. Shortly after the Whalers took the NHL with them, minor league hockey showed up in the form of the New York Rangers affiliate, the Hartford Wolf Pack. The Wolf Pack has kept hockey alive and well in Hartford, and their games at the XL Center are a great night out for fans and newcomers to the sport alike. If you're looking for a family-friendly, affordable night out, you may want to consider an action-packed night of hockey. It is a great chance to check out some of the future stars of the NHL as well.

225 Trumbull St., 860-762-6451
hartfordwolfpack.com

PLAY A ROUND
AT GOODWIN AND KENEY PARK GOLF COURSES

The Greater Hartford area has its fair share of golf courses, and Hartford itself is home to the newly refurbished Keney and Goodwin Park golf courses. Goodwin Park is a twenty-seven-hole facility that has been hosting area golfers since 1906. It features a championship- level, eighteen-hole, par 70 course for those looking for a full round and also features the nine-hole North course for beginners and those looking to play a quick nine. Keney Park was recently reopened in the spring of 2016, after extensive restoration, which included a consulting partnership with the PGA. Both of these gems have quickly become go-to courses for golf enthusiasts from all over the state.

Goodwin Park Golf Course, 1130 Maple Ave., 860-543-8518
goodwinparkgolfcourse.com

Keney Park Golf Course, 280 Tower Ave., 860-543-8618
keneyparkgolfcourse.com

71

WATCH
A VINTAGE BASEBALL GAME

There's really nothing like taking in a live baseball game. There's something even more special about watching live baseball played with the rules, equipment, and costumes of the 19th century. To say baseball has changed over the last 150 years is an understatement, and the Friends of Vintage Baseball work to maintain the history of the earliest incarnation of the national pastime. Games are usually played in Colt Park, are free to the public, and teams from all over the Northeast play in front of enthusiastic baseball fans and history buffs alike. Even if you think you know the sport of baseball inside and out, you may still be in for a pleasant surprise watching the game played by Civil War-era rules.

Colt Park
friendsofvintagebaseball.org

©Hartford Business Improvement District

72

TAKE A STROLL
THROUGH BUSHNELL PARK

Amidst the hustle and bustle of downtown Hartford exists roughly fifty acres of green space known as Bushnell Park. The oldest publicly funded park in the United States, it features winding paths with clusters of large trees, a pond, and several historical monuments and structures. Listed on the National Register of Historic Places, the park was originally opened in 1868 and is annually the host for almost every major outdoor event and festival in the city. It's also the perfect oasis in an urban landscape, allowing visitors to peacefully picnic, practice yoga, or simply get away from it all. In the autumn months the park's trees are alight with color, whereas in the springtime the colorful blossoms give the entire downtown an ambiance of awakening.

bushnellpark.org

CULTURE AND HISTORY

VISIT THE OLDEST CONTINUOUSLY OPERATING

PUBLIC ART MUSEUM

Founded in 1842, the Wadsworth Atheneum Museum of Art is a national treasure. Considered the first public art institution in the United States, the Wadsworth was also the first museum in the country to start collecting contemporary American art. Their collection of European, American, and contemporary art, alongside decorative arts, costumes, and textiles, is second to none. Spend a day touring the gorgeous halls and gaze upon works by Monet, Picasso, Gauguin, Renoir, O'Keeffe, and dozens upon dozens of other world-renowned artists. Take part in one of their many guided tours or stroll around at your own leisure. Either way, with multiple floors filled with hundreds of years' worth of beautiful and intriguing artwork, the Wadsworth is a must for anyone visiting Hartford.

600 Main St., 860-278-2670
thewadsworth.org

TIP

The Wadsworth also houses a stunning theater. Check their website for a complete schedule of film screenings and special events held there.

MARK TWAIN
SAMUEL L. CLEMENS
1835 1910

TOUR THE HOME
OF MARK TWAIN

From 1874 to 1891, Samuel Clemens (a.k.a. Mark Twain) and his family lived in the stylishly ornate home still standing today on Farmington Avenue in Hartford. Now a testament to one of America's greatest writers, The Mark Twain House & Museum offers visitors a glimpse into the life and times of Twain. Offering living history tours of the house itself and a forty-five-thousand-square-foot museum adjacent to the home, this facility puts the historic house and the author's legacy on display for all to see. The Mark Twain House & Museum also offers a range of unique events. From readings by best-selling authors to ghost tours and live performances, there is always something worth checking out at the Twain House.

351 Farmington Ave., 860-247-0998
marktwainhouse.org

SPEND THE DAY
AT CEDAR HILL CEMETERY

Cemeteries sometimes get a bad reputation thanks to horror movies and campfire ghost stories. But not every cemetery is a creepy, run-down, ghost-infested field. Take Cedar Hill Cemetery, for example. Established in 1864, Cedar Hill is over 270 acres of pristine landscaped woodlands, waterways, and some of the most ornate memorials you'll find anywhere. Not only that, but the Cedar Hill Cemetery Foundation schedules a variety of events at the cemetery including live music, scavenger hunts, movie nights, and various themed tours, among other things.

453 Fairfield Ave., 860-956-3311
cedarhillfoundation.org

TIP

Tour Cedar Hill and search out the headstones of the many famous Connecticut residents buried there, including legendary actress Katharine Hepburn, Samuel Colt, founder of Colt Industries and inventor of the famous Colt 45 revolver; and the world-famous financier and philanthropist J. P. Morgan.

WATCH THE DRAGON BOAT RACES
AND TAKE IN THE ASIAN FESTIVAL

Riverfront Recapture's annual Riverfront Dragon Boat & Asian Festival takes place every August along the Connecticut River. It's a free, family-friendly, and unique celebration of all the various Asian cultures that have settled in the greater Hartford area. Featuring authentic Asian music, dance performances, food vendors, martial arts expos, and, of course, Dragon Boat races, this is an excellent way to spend a summer Saturday. There is something almost otherworldly about watching human-powered boats with decorative Chinese dragon heads and tails hurtling down an urban river. While the races are certainly one highlight, the entertainment inspired by various cultures from China, Japan, Mongolia, Korea, and more make the trip a worthwhile experience. It comes as no surprise that this event was named one of the "Top 10 Dragon Boat Festivals in the United States."

300 Columbus Blvd., 860-713-3131
riverfront.org/events/dragon-boat-asian-festival

PLAY WITH ALL THE STUFF
AT THE CONNECTICUT SCIENCE CENTER

You've probably heard the expression "fun for all ages" a million times. But the Connecticut Science Center truly embodies that sentiment. With over one hundred hands-on exhibits, both permanent to the museum and otherwise, the Science Center offers a world of exploration that children and adults will find both fun and informative. From physics to paleontology to astronomy, and just about every other discipline in between, the Science Center covers a vast assortment of topics and delivers them as a highly enjoyable user experience. Throw in a 3D theater that brings nature to life on screen, live stage shows that provide for audience interaction with science, and a bevy of other special events, and you have. undoubtedly one of the more unique attractions Hartford has to offer.

250 Columbus Blvd., 860-724-3623
CTScienceCenter.org

78

EMBRACE THE ARTS
AT REAL ART WAYS

It would not be a stretch to call Real Art Ways one of the leading contemporary arts organizations in the country. This Hartford institution has a diverse lineup of programs and exhibits that touch on virtually all artistic disciplines, sometimes simultaneously on any given night of the week. Their galleries are open daily and display innovative visual art exhibitions from local and international artists. Their cinema, also open seven nights a week, features cutting-edge independent film culled from all over the world. Real Art Ways also presents amazing musical performances, literary events, spoken word performances, and community-based programming as well. There is always something amazing happening at Real Art Ways.

56 Arbor St., 860-232-1006
realartways.org

TIP

The third Thursday of every month is a special time at Real Art Ways as they present their popular Creative Cocktail Hour. Go for the art and music; stay for the interesting and friendly people.

79

BE AMAZED
BY THE BEAUTY OF NIGHT FALL

Every October, for one magical evening, a Hartford park is transformed into a living art installation that features music, dance, theater, spoken word, elaborate costumes, and giant puppets. Night Fall has quickly become a must-attend event and one of Hartford's most talked about artistic treasures. Artist Anne Cubberly creates distinctive and amazingly massive puppets that are complemented by outstanding regional talent from almost every artistic discipline imaginable. There are also food trucks, vendors, artmaking stations, and various side shows that give the whole thing a festive atmosphere. In the weeks leading up to Night Fall, there are free art workshops held across the city, and Night Fall artists work with people to design and create lanterns that wind up being part of the procession that is the centerpiece of the entire performance.

nightfallhartford.org

80

READ THE BRICKS
ON PRATT STREET

Walking up and down a city block with your head down, staring at the sidewalk doesn't sound like much fun, unless you are on Pratt Street in Hartford. In 1988, in an effort to raise money for street improvements, bricks were sold at $45 each and could be inscribed with just about anything you could fit on a brick. While most of the bricks are messages to loved ones, memorials, and advertisements, there are dozens of bricks with quirky messages like, "I Can See Up Your Skirt." As if Pratt Street wasn't unique enough amongst other downtown blocks, these bricks and their often cheeky messages add a certain charm you really won't find anywhere else.

ATTEND (OR MARCH IN) A PARADE

Hartford and the surrounding towns have an amazingly diverse mixture of cultures that call the area home. There are some estimates that put the number of languages spoken in Hartford above eighty. With so many different cultures, there are bound to be some pretty unique cultural celebrations. For almost the entire calendar year, Hartford is home to myriad parades. Some of the highlights include the St. Patrick's Day Parade, Puerto Rican Parade, and West Indian Independence Celebration. This is a city that is proud of its cultural diversity, and what better way to show that off than to march proudly through the streets of downtown.

Hartford.com/events

82

VISIT
THE HARRIET BEECHER STOWE CENTER

Abraham Lincoln once called her "the little woman who wrote the book that made this great war." In 1852, Harriet Beecher Stowe changed the world with her best-selling anti-slavery novel, *Uncle Tom's Cabin*. The Harriet Beecher Stowe Center not only preserves Stowe's Hartford home but offers a riveting look back at the life and times of one of America's heroes in the anti-slavery movement. But the Stowe Center is more than just a standout museum preserving the history of one of Connecticut's favorite daughters. Their events and programming run the gamut, from after-dark tours highlighting 19th-century spiritualism to social education programs, as they continue to spread Stowe's message of compassion and equality.

77 Forest St., 860-522-9258
harrietbeecherstowe.org

GET A TASTE
OF THE CARIBBEAN

For over a decade the annual Taste of the Caribbean & Jerk Festival has been a vibrant and pulsating celebration of all aspects of Caribbean culture. The festival represents all of the English-, Spanish-, and French- speaking Caribbean nations that are embodied by thousands of Hartford area residents. With attendee estimates hitting twenty thousand in recent years, this event has proved to be one of Hartford's biggest and brightest cultural celebrations. The festival includes danceable music, vendors, children's activities, and of course, lots of amazing food. The Taste of the Caribbean & Jerk Festival takes place in August every year at the Mortensen Riverfront Plaza in downtown Hartford.

300 Columbus Blvd., 860-306-1693
tastect.org

TOUR
THE ARCH IN BUSHNELL PARK

One of Hartford's most recognizable landmarks is the Soldiers and Sailors Memorial Arch in Bushnell Park. Originally dedicated on September 17, 1886, the twenty-fourth anniversary of the Battle of Antietam, the arch was built to honor the more than four thousand Hartford citizens who served in the Civil War (including roughly four hundred souls who perished during the war). From the outside the arch is a gorgeous Gothic-style monument complete with scenes from the Civil War and eight-foot-tall statues representing different people who left their lives behind to fight for the Union. But the real fun is taking a tour of the inside. Every Thursday afternoon from May through October (and different hours by appointment), guides offer informational tours that shed new light on the classic structure.

Bushnell Park, 860-232-6710
bushnellpark.org

TAKE
A SCULPTURE WALK

One of the newest additions to the cultural landscape of Hartford is the Lincoln Financial Sculpture Walk. Along the banks of the Connecticut River sit sixteen tremendous works of art, many of which celebrate the life and accomplishments of Abraham Lincoln. But this isn't just a tour for history buffs. All art lovers are encouraged to stroll the Riverfront area and enjoy large-scale sculptures and murals set against a bucolic oasis in the heart of the city. Each one of the official works of art included in the tour gives a description of the piece and its meaning. Mobile tours and printable maps are available through the Riverfront Recapture website.

860-713-3131
riverfront.org/parks/art-in-parks

VISIT
THE BUTLER-MCCOOK HOUSE

Nestled among the modern steel and stone structures along Main Street, there is a landmark that's been witness to over 230 years of Hartford history. Originally built in 1782, the Butler-McCook House is a living time capsule featuring original furnishings from the Colonial and Victorian eras. Behind the home lies the Victorian-style ornamental garden, which stands as a peaceful refuge from the surrounding urban landscape. Also held within the Butler-McCook House is the Main Street History Center. Using the observations and experiences of the Butler and McCook families to give a detailed history of Hartford's downtown, this exhibit is a must for anyone looking for a direct window into some of Hartford's unique past.

396 Main St., 860-522-1806
ctlandmarks.org

VISIT EBK GALLERY

The old adage about big things coming in small packages is true, especially when talking about EBK Gallery. Located inside the historic Goodwin Building in downtown Hartford, EBK Gallery continuously presents contemporary works of art from local, national, and international artists. Meant to be an introduction to an artist's larger body of work, EBK Gallery is the perfect complement to a night out or supplement to your artistic travels around the city. With all of the artwork on display also for sale, EBK Gallery also provides a serendipitous opportunity for those looking to acquire a unique piece of contemporary art. Make sure to pay attention to the EBK Gallery's list of events for their art receptions that accompany each new exhibition.

218 Pearl St., 860-523-9384
ebkgallery.com

VISIT THE OLDEST HISTORIC SITE
IN HARTFORD

Originally plotted out in 1640, four years after the first English settlers arrived, the Ancient Burying Ground is the only surviving testament to the colonists of the 1600s. It is replete with history, as it was Hartford's most prominent place to be buried until sometime in the early 1800s. While its present size is a fraction of what it was while it was still in use, the Ancient Burying Ground still serves as the final resting place for some of Hartford's earliest citizens. There are still 415 stones visible to visitors, and all of them are prime examples of 17th- and 18th-century interment designs. Guided tours of the Ancient Burying Ground are available, but visitors are advised that stone rubbings are not permitted.

60 Gold St.
theancientburyingground.org

TAKE A TOUR
OF THE STATE CAPITOL

One of the more important and opulent buildings in Hartford is the State Capitol, and it's open to the public for both guided and self-guided tours. Highlights include the Connecticut Hall of Fame, the Hall of Flags (which includes various flags carried into battle by Connecticut soldiers), and various other items of importance to both Connecticut and U.S. history. Tours also provide in-depth information about the State Capitol building itself, which is a national historic landmark. State Capitol tours also include the CT house and Senate Chambers, as well as the adjacent Legislative Office Building. Guided tours are available year-round on weekdays between 9:00 a.m. and 1:00 p.m. Self-guided tours are available during normal business hours, Monday through Friday.

210 Capitol Ave., #3, 860-240-0222
cga.ct.gov/capitoltours

TOUR
THE CONNECTICUT HISTORICAL SOCIETY MUSEUM

The official historical society for the entire state of Connecticut naturally resides in the state's capital. The Connecticut Historical Society lives inside a Colonial Revival mansion originally owned by inventor Curtis Veeder (who invented an assortment of mechanical apparatuses). This massive structure is now the home of an amalgam of Connecticut history. Highlights include a four-hundred-year interactive timeline made up of over five hundred objects on display. Their collection also includes an entire room dedicated to inn and tavern signs dating as far back as pre–Revolutionary War Connecticut. Special exhibits are always popping up throughout the year as well, focusing on various artistic, social, and cultural themes. This is a must-stop for anyone wanting to learn more about Connecticut and U.S. history.

1 Elizabeth St., 860-236-5621
chs.org

VISIT
THE JOSELOFF GALLERY

Located in the Harry Jack Gray Center on the University of Hartford campus, the Joseloff Gallery exhibits works of contemporary art in virtually all media. The gallery centers on works created by students enrolled at the Hartford Art School at the University of Hartford (specifically the Alexander A. Goldfarb Student Exhibition) and other renowned regional, national, and international artists. The Joseloff Gallery is an exciting glimpse into the past, present, and future of contemporary art. Since its inception in 1989, the Joseloff Gallery has quickly grown into one of the most respected university galleries of its size in the country. All exhibits at the Joseloff Gallery are free and open to the public.

200 Bloomfield Ave., 860-768-4090
joseloffgallery.org

92

EXPLORE
THE MUSEUM OF CONNECTICUT HISTORY

Being a state capital has its perks. The Connecticut State Library houses the impressive Museum of Connecticut History, which holds several permanent and rotating exhibits that focus on the governmental, military, and industrial history of the Nutmeg State. Six days a week the museum offers visitors a free chance to come face to face with Connecticut's role in major events in U.S. history. The Memorial Hall features portraits of seventy-two different Connecticut governors dating back to pre–Revolutionary War days. Possibly the gem of this assemblage of artifacts, though, is the Colt Firearms Collection. The collection features a massive display of firearms produced at the facility owned by Samuel Colt in Hartford, dating back to the 1830s. This exhibit alone is a must-see for history buffs.

231 Capitol Ave., 860-757-6521
museumofcthistory.org

TOUR
THE COLTSVILLE NATIONAL HISTORIC PARK

Originally designated as a National Historic Landmark in 2008, the Coltsville section of Hartford is comprised of the former factory, working houses, and residences owned by innovator and manufacturing pioneer Samuel Colt. The area was recently designated a National Historic Park, and official walking tours began in 2016. The tour of the park only takes about an hour, but the amount of Hartford, Connecticut, and U.S. history is a veritable smorgasbord. The new National Park is still in its infancy, and big plans are afoot, but for the time being feel free to stroll Colt Park and the surrounding area while the story of Samuel Colt, his family, and his factory unfolds before you.

106 Wethersfield Ave.
hartford.gov/parks/193-colt-park

94

VISIT THE HARTFORD HISTORY CENTER

AT THE LIBRARY

Located on the third floor of the gorgeous Downtown Hartford Public Library, the Hartford History Center provides a multidimensional view of Hartford's history that is both engaging and interactive. Featuring an art walk with a rotating display of original works and a bevy of exhibitions and presentations, the Hartford History Center is not your run-of-the-mill museum. History is presented through various artistic mediums, including a multimedia collection featuring over one hundred thousand printed materials. The Hartford History Center is open to the general public. However, there are some rules governing the use of the printed materials in order to maintain their integrity. But if you're looking for a chance to scour through hundreds of years' worth of books, photos, manuscripts, and various ephemera, then these rules are well worth it.

500 Main St., 860-695-6300
http://hhc.hplct.org

LOVE
HARTFORD

SHOPPING AND FASHION

95

SHOP LOCAL
AT HARTFORD PRINTS!

Ask any of the Sisters Gale what the main purpose of their Hartford Prints! brand is and they'll be happy to tell you that it's all about "handmade and homegrown." Originally begun with the creation of letterpress stationery, Hartford Prints! has grown into a brick-and-mortar shop featuring stationery, clothing, and a wide array of locally created goods. Everything in their quaint boutique is handmade in-store or in collaboration with other local designers. It's clear that everything inside Hartford Prints! is not just handmade, but also made with love. You'll also be hard pressed to find any hipper Connecticut-branded apparel around, including their popular "Small State, Big Heart" line of products.

42½ Pratt St., 860-578-8447
hartfordprints.com

TIP

Love what Hartford Prints! does and wonder how they do it? You're in luck. Attend one of their varied workshop offerings to learn more about letterpress and/or other artistic endeavors hosted by guest designers.

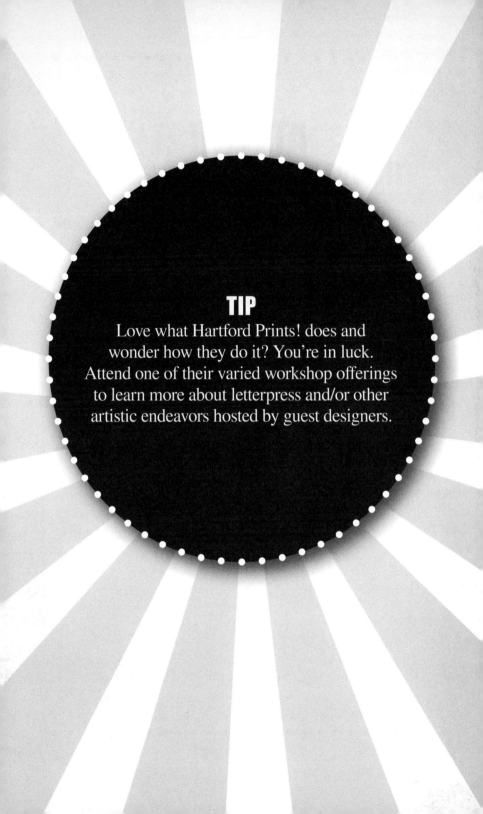

ATTEND
THE TRASHION FASHION SHOW

When you think of fashion shows and fashion in general, the first thing that comes to mind is probably not what's sitting out in your recycle bin. Then again, you're not Amy Merli, founder of Trashion Fashion, who decided to combine her love of style with her passion for environmentalism. The annual Trashion Fashion show is a choreographed runway that features wearable art made from materials normally found in recycling centers and (unfortunately) landfills. You will never see plastic bags, bottles, and various paper goods look so chic, all while raising awareness for just how much stuff we throw away. Held in Hartford right around Earth Day every year, the Trashion Fashion show is a must-see event for a great cause.

929-500-2128
trashionfashion.org

PURCHASE JEANS
THAT WILL LAST A LIFETIME

It says it right in their name, but the Hartford Denim Company specializes in all things denim. Utilizing traditional techniques, the finest materials available, and even antique industrial sewing machines, it's safe to say that you may never again own a pair of pants quite like this. Their clothes are as comfortable as they are strong, and Hartford Denim backs every purchase with free repairs for the life of the garment. You may literally never have to buy another pair of jeans again. Everything Hartford Denim Company produces is cut and sewn right in their shop in Hartford, so not only are you buying a great garment, you're supporting local manufacturing as well.

30 Bartholomew Ave., 860-880-0495
hartforddenimcompany.com

98

STEP UP
TO THE (CAMERA) BAR

For over fifty years Camera Bar has been a fixture in downtown Hartford. As you would guess by their name, Camera Bar sells cameras. Lots of cameras. Camera Bar is a unique shopping experience for a variety of reasons, not the least of which is that they still sell, repair, and process film for APS, 35mm, and 120mm cameras. Camera Bar is one of the last places around where you can get actual film developed. If you are an amateur photographer (or pro) dabbling in film yourself, they have everything you need, including darkroom supplies. Not interested in revisiting the not-too-distant past? That's okay. Camera Bar is still the best place around to find your new favorite digital camera too.

75 Asylum St., 860-525-2159
camerabar.com

TREAT YOURSELF
AT A FASHION LANDMARK

For over a hundred years, Stackpole in Hartford has been the go-to name in quality fashion. Located right in the heart of downtown Hartford is Stackpole Moore Tryon, a renowned independent clothing retailer with a long and storied history. Stackpole features custom-made suits and designer wear for both men and women, along with a wide selection of items from some of the region's top fashion designers. Stackpole has been voted the area's best retailer for both men's and women's clothing by *Hartford Magazine* and *Connecticut Magazine*. Their longtime location is also supplemented by the Stackpole Moore Tryon Tuesday's outlet store, which is situated just around the corner. The outlet features past-season and overstock styles for both men and women at discounted prices.

242 Trumbull St., 860-522-0181
stackpolemooretryon.com

SLIP INTO A PAIR
FROM THE BROTHERS CRISP

In an old factory building in the Parkville section of Hartford, one company is looking to become the leading manufacturer of handmade footwear. The Brothers Crisp are cobblers first and foremost, designing and producing their own line of stylish footwear. Using techniques that date as far back as the 19th century, the Brothers Crisp produces a line that includes high-top sneakers, moccasins, slippers, and boots of various styles. Footwear can also be made to order as well. While the shoes are on the pricier end of the scale, there's really no substitute for handcrafted items made with quality techniques and materials. Shoes come in full sizes, and if you can't make the trip to their shop, the Brothers Crisp will ship worldwide.

1477 Park St., Suite 2E, 860-385-2040
thebrotherscrisp.com

SUGGESTED ITINERARIES

FOR THE ART LOVERS

Take a Sculpture Walk, 111

Race in the Art Sled Derby, 78

Visit the Joseloff Gallery, 118

Embrace the Arts at Real Art Ways, 102

Visit EBK Gallery, 114

Visit the Oldest Continuously Operating Public Art Museum, 92

FOODIES HEAD FOR THE SOUTH END

Experience a Taste of Peru at Piolin, 33

Spoil Your Dinner with Italian Cookies and Pastries at Mozzicato's, 8

Grab a Grinder from Franklin Giant Sandwich Shop, 40

Make a Stop at The First & Last Tavern, 38

Stock Up on Pasta at Difiore, 28

Visit the Spanish Coastline via Costa del Sol, 30

Experience a Taste of Colombia at La Fonda, 35

Spend an Evening at Casona, 47

Purchase Some Sausage from LaRosa's, 44

Have Brunch at the Place 2 Be, 45

THERE'S ALWAYS MUSIC IN THE AIR

Attend a Hartford Symphony Orchestra Performance, 61

Acquire a New Appreciation for Opera, 57

Attend the Greater Hartford Festival of Jazz, 63

Make Mondays Fun with Free Jazz in the Park, 52

Hang Out at Sully's Pub, 70

Get the Blues at Black-Eyed Sally's, 56

Chill at the Black-Eyed & Blues Fest, 67

Enjoy the Music at Infinity Hall, 59

Experience the Trinity International Hip-Hop Festival, 72

HISTORY BUFFS UNITE

Visit the Harriet Beecher Stowe Center, 107

Tour the Home of Mark Twain, 95

Visit the Butler-McCook House, 113

Tour the Arch in Bushnell Park, 109

Spend the Day at Cedar Hill Cemetery, 96

Visit the Oldest Historic Site in Hartford, 115

Visit the Hartford History Center at the Library, 121

Take a Tour of the State Capitol, 116

Tour the Connecticut Historical Society Museum, 117

Tour the Coltsville National Historic Park, 120

Explore the Museum of Connecticut History, 119

GET SOME FRESH AIR

Play a Round at Goodwin and Keney Park Golf Courses, 86

Spend the Day in Elizabeth Park, 82

Watch a Vintage Baseball Game, 87

Take a Sculpture Walk, 111

Take a Stroll through Bushnell Park, 89

Cruise along the Connecticut River, 83

Read the Bricks on Pratt Street, 105

FUN FOR THE WHOLE FAMILY

Hit Up a Comic-Con, or Two, 68

Eat a Big Amount of Little Donuts, 18

Heed the Call of the Pipes, 58

Get a Taste of the Caribbean, 108

Play with All the Stuff at the Connecticut Science Center, 101
Celebrate Hartford and a Hooker, 75
Be Amazed by the Beauty of Night Fall, 104
Ride the Bushnell Park Carousel, 81
Attend (or March in) a Parade, 106
Ice Skate in Bushnell Park during Winterfest, 79
Watch the Dragon Boat Races and Take in the Asian Festival, 99

THE PERFORMING ARTS ARE ALIVE

See a Show at TheaterWorks, Too, 55
Attend a Hartt School Performance, 69
See a Show at Hartford Stage, 54
Experience a TNMoT AZTRo Performance, 60
Experience a Show at the Bushnell, 50
Attend a Performance at the Academy of the Arts, 66
Immerse Yourself in Improv, 51
Experience a Show at HartBeat Ensemble, 65

DOWNTOWN DINING

Grab a Pint at Vaughan's Public House, 12
Eat Korean Barbeque at Sunberry, 3

Grab Some Sushi at Feng, 14

Get a Quick Bite at One of the Kitchens, 37

Grab a Beer at City Steam, 24

Sip Wine at Bin228, 23

Mangiare a Sorella, 20

Grab a Dog at Woody's, 36

Spend an Evening at the Russell, 43

Experience a Meal at On20, 32

EVENTS
BY SEASON

SPRING

Experience the Trinity International Hip-Hop Festival, 72

Attend a Film Festival, or Two, 73

Celebrate Hartford and a Hooker, 75

Attend the Trashion Fashion Show, 126

SUMMER

Make Mondays Fun with Free Jazz in the Park, 52

Attend the Greater Hartford Festival of Jazz, 63

Chill at the Black-Eyed & Blues Fest, 67

Hit Up a Comic-Con, or Two, 68

Cruise along the Connecticut River, 83

Watch a Vintage Baseball Game, 87

Watch the Dragon Boat Races and Take in the Asian Festival, 99

Get a Taste of the Caribbean, 108

AUTUMN

Heed the Call of the Pipes, 58

Spend the Day at Cedar Hill Cemetery, 96

Be Amazed by the Beauty of Night Fall, 104

Visit the Oldest Historic Site in Hartford, 115

WINTER

Race in the Art Sled Derby, 78

Ice Skate in Bushnell Park during Winterfest, 79

Cheer on the Huskies at a UConn Basketball Game, 84

Attend a Wolf Pack Game, 85

INDEX

Abyssinian Ethiopian, 41

Ancient Burying Ground, 115

Bear's Smokehouse, 26

bin228, 23, 135

Black-Eyed & Blues Fest, 67, 132, 137

Black-Eyed Sally's, 56, 67, 132

Brazil Grill, 46

Brew HaHa Comedy Club, 25

Brothers Crisp, 130

Bushnell Center for the Performing Arts, 50

Bushnell Park, 52, 63, 67, 75, 79, 81, 89, 109, 132, 133, 134, 138

Bushnell Park Carousel, 81, 134

Butler-McCook House, 113, 132

Camera Bar, 128

Casona, 47, 132

Cedar Hill Cemetery, 96–97, 132, 138

Charter Oak Cultural Center, 53

Cinestudio, 64

City Steam, 24–25, 135
Colt Firearms Exhibit, 119
Coltsville National Historic Park, 120, 133
ConnectiCon, 68
Connecticut Historical Society, 117, 133
Connecticut River, 32, 83, 99, 111, 133, 137
Connecticut Science Center, 101, 134
Connecticut State Capitol Building, 116, 133
Connecticut State Library, 119
Costa del Sol, 30, 131
Coyote Flaco, 27
Difiore Ravioli Shop, 28, 131
Dragon Boat Races & Asian Festival, 99, 134
EBK Gallery, 114, 131
El Mercado, 6
El Nuevo Serape Restaurant, 27
Elizabeth Park, 78, 82, 133
Feng Asian Bistro, 14
Fire & Spice, 17
Firebox Restaurant, 4

First & Last Tavern, 38, 131

Franklin Giant Sandwich Shop, 40, 131

Friends of Vintage Baseball, 87

Goodwin Golf Course, 86, 133

Greater Hartford Academy of the Arts, 66

Greater Hartford Festival of Jazz, 63, 132, 137

Hanging Hills Brewing Company, 42

Harriet Beecher Stowe Center, 107, 132

Hartford Art Sled Derby, 78

Hartford Belle Riverboat Cruises, 83

Hartford ComiConn, 68

Hartford Denim Company, 127

Hartford Flavor Company, 34

Hartford History Center at Hartford Public Library, 121, 133

Hartford Jewish Film Festival, 73

Hartford Opera Theater, 57

Hartford Prints!, 124–125

Hartford Stage, 54, 134

Hartford Symphony Orchestra, 50, 61, 132

Hartford Wolf Pack, 85

HartBeat Ensemble, 65, 134
Hartt School, 69, 134
Hooker Day, 75
Ice Skating, 79
Infinity Hall, 59, 132
Jazz in the Park, 52, 132, 137
Joseloff Gallery, 118, 131
Keney Golf Course, 86, 133
King & I Thai, 7
Kitchen at Billings Forge, the, 37
Kitchen at Hartford Public Library, the, 37
Know Good Market, 31
La Fonda, 35, 131
LaRosa's, 44, 132
Little River Restoratives, 16
Mark Twain House, 95, 132
Mo's Midtown, 10–11
Monte Alban Restaurant, 27
Mozzicato DePasquale Bakery and Pastry Shop, 8–9, 131
Night Fall, 104, 134, 138

On20, 32, 135

Out Film CT, 73

Piolin, 33, 131

Pipes in the Valley, 58

Place 2 Be, the, 45, 132

Polish National Home, 13

Pratt Street Bricks, 105, 133

Puerto Rican Parade, 106

Real Art Ways, 60, 102–103, 131

Reel Youth Hartford Film Festival, 73

Russell, the, 43, 135

Scotts' Jamaican Bakery, 22

Sculpture Walk, 111, 131, 133

Sea Tea Improv, 51

Soldiers and Sailors Memorial Arch, 109

Sorella, 20–21, 135

Spigot Cafe, 29

St. Patrick's Day Parade, 106

Stackpole, 129

Sully's Pub, 70, 132

Sunberry, 3, 134

Tangiers International Market, 2

Taste of Caribbean & Jerk Festival, 108, 134, 137

Tastease, 18

TheaterWorks, 55, 134

Tisane Euro-Asian Café, 19

TNMoT AZTRo, 60, 134

Trashion Fashion Show, 126, 137

Trinity Film Festival, 73

Trinity Hip-Hop Festival, 72

UConn Basketball, 84 138

Vaughan's Public House, 12, 134

Wadsworth Atheneum, 60, 61, 92

West Indian Independence Celebration, 60

Woody's, 36, 135

Winterfest, 79, 134, 138